MEMOIRS

OF THE

GEOLOGICAL SURVEY

OF

GREAT BRITAIN,

AND OF THE

MUSEUM OF PRACTICAL GEOLOGY.

GEOLOGY OF PARTS OF

WILTSHIRE AND GLOUCESTERSHIRE.

(SHEET 34.)

BY

A. C. RAMSAY, F.R.S., F.G.S., Local Director,

W. T. AVELINE, F.G.S., and EDWARD HULL, B.A., F.G.S.

LISTS OF FOSSILS BY ROBERT ETHERIDGE, F.R.S.E., F.G.S.

PUBLISHED BY ORDER OF THE LORDS COMMISSIONERS OF HER MAJESTY'S TREASURY.

LONDON:

PRINTED FOR HER MAJESTY'S STATIONERY OFFICE;

PUBLISHED BY

LONGMAN, BROWN, GREEN, AND LONGMANS.

1858.

NOTICE.

I TRUST that the accompanying Memoir will prove acceptable to the Public, and especially to the Landowners and Agriculturists in those parts of Wiltshire and Gloucestershire, the geological relations of which are described in Sheet 34.

RODERICK I. MURCHISON,
Director General.

Nov. 10, 1858.

THE country mapped in Sheet No. 34 consists of a series of formations from the Lower Lias of Stroud Valley up to the Plastic clay of Marlborough Downs and Aldbourn Chase. Of these, the Oolite and Cretaceous rocks near Corsham and Calne, and all the Upper Cretaceous and Tertiary rocks, were surveyed by Mr. W. T. Aveline; and part of the Lower Greensand, and all the remaining Oolites down to the Lias, by Mr. E. Hull, forming the greater part of the Sheet. The larger part of the Memoir is by Mr. Hull, who contributes the descriptions of the Lias and Oolite rocks (excepting at Swindon). The Cretaceous and Eocene strata are described by Mr. Aveline; and the Portland and Purbeck beds, and the Grey Wethers, by myself. The lists of fossils are by Mr. Etheridge.

A. C. RAMSAY,
Local Director of the Geological
Survey of Great Britain.

CONTENTS.

GEOLOGY OF PARTS OF WILTSHIRE AND GLOUCESTERSHIRE.

(SHEET 34.)

PHYSICAL FEATURES OF THE LIASSIC AND OOLITIC DISTRICTS.

THIS area may be described as part of an elevated plain or table-land, with a general south-easterly slope towards the base of the Chalk escarpment. It rises gradually towards the north and west, and is abruptly terminated by the Oolitic escarpment which overlooks the vale of the Severn. The direction of this escarpment is shown in Sheets 35 and 44. It forms the boundary of the Cotteswold Hills. Of the numerous valleys by which this table-land is intersected some of the most beautiful enter the district under consideration in the country round Stroud, at the north-west corner of the Sheet, and present valuable sections of the strata, as they crop out along their flanks.

The central portion of the table-land is traversed by several parallel minor ridges, trending from the south-west to the north-east. They are formed of limestones, viz., the great Oolite,* Cornbrash,† and Coralline oolite‡; while the intervening hollows consist of the Oxford and Kimmeridge clays. It is to be observed, however, that the Oxford clay in some places rises higher than the Cornbrash at the line of junction. The bands of limestone are usually cultivated for grain, while the clays form meadows and pasture lands.

Overlooking the broad oolitic plain there rises a second escarpment formed of the Chalk. Between Cherhill and Compton Beauchamp it trends in a sinuous line from south-west to north-east, and the plain immediately at its base consists chiefly of Gault and Kimmeridge clay. The Chalk itself in

* Marked g^7 in the Geological Survey Sheets.
† " g^8 " "
‡ " g^{11} " "

this Sheet consists partly of two escarpments, more particularly described at page 37. Marlborough Downs, and the country east and north-east of Ogbourne St. George, form the upper escarpment.

It will save repetition to mention that the general dip of the strata is towards the south-east, at angles varying from 1 to 3 degrees. The formations are described in ascending order.

Geological Formations.

Lias.

Lower Lias.—The existence of this formation in Sheet 34, is inferred from the occurrence of marshy ground at the base of the Marlstone. It occupies a very small area at the entrance of Stroud valley, and is marked g^1.

Characteristic Fossils of the Lower Lias (g^1).

Echinodermata.

Acrosalenia crinifera. Quenst.

Brachiopoda.

Spirifer Walcottii. Sow.
„ rostratus. Schloth.
Terebratula numismalis. Lam.
Rhynchonella rimosa. Buch.

Conchifera.

Plicatula spinosa. Sow.
Gryphæa incurva. Sow.
Pecten novemcostæ. Sow.
Lima pectinoides. Sow.
„ gigantea. Sow.
Crenatula ventricosa. Sow.
Modiola minima. Sow.
„ cuneata. Sow.
Area truncata. Sow.
Trifonia litterata, Phill.
Cardinia attenuata. Stuch.
„ hybrida. Stuch.
„ Listeri. Stuch.
Hippopodium ponderosum. Sow.
Nucula complanata. Phill.
Leda ovum. Sow.

Gasteropoda.

Pleurotomaria Anglica. Sow.
Trochus imbricatus. Sow.

Cephalopoda.

Ammonites Henleyi. Sow.
„ communis. Sow.
„ planicostatus. Sow.
„ obtusus. Sow.

Marlstone.—This formation (marked g^2) forms small tabulated promontories along the flanks of the Oolitic escarpment, examples of which may be seen around Stroud.

It consists of two parts; an upper rock bed of ferrugino-calcareous sandstone, resting on a series of soft sands of various colours, with nodular masses of impure limestone and balls of concretionary iron ore. It usually becomes more clayey towards the base, and passes imperceptibly into the Lower Lias clay. The top bed is frequently a hard limestone, a few inches thick, containing *Rhynchonella variabilis* in great abundance, and in some places *Ammonites annulatus*.

CHARACTERISTIC FOSSILS OF THE MARLSTONE, g^2.

Brachiopoda.

Terebratula quadrifida. Lam.
„ punctata. Sow.
„ resupinata.
Rhynchonella acuta. Sow.
„ tetrahedra. Sow.
„ variabilis. Schloth.
Lingula Beanii. Phill.

Conchifera.

Gryphæa gigantea. Sow.
Pecten sublævis. Phill.
„ æquivalvis. Sow.
„ cinctus. Sow.
„ cingulatus. Goldf.
Plicatula spinosa. Sow.
Avicula novemcostæ. Brown.
Lima punctata. Sow.
Modiola cuneata. Sow.
„ scalprum. Sow.
Cardium truncatum. Sow.
Unicardium cardioidès. Phill.
Cardinia concinna. Stuch.
Myacites unionoides.
Pholadomya ambigua. Sow.

Gasteropoda.

Pleurotomaria expansa. Sow.

Echinodermata.

Uraster Gaveyi. Forbes.
Ophiura Egertoni.

Cephalopoda.

Ammonites fimbriatus. Sow.
„ annulatus Sow.
„ rotiformis. Sow.
„ margaritatus. Montf.
„ spinatus. Brug.
„ Planicostatus. Sow.
Belemnites elongatus. Miller.
„ arcuarius. Schloth.
Nautilus truncatus. Sow.

Upper Lias Clay and Sand.—These strata compose the flanks of the valleys which ramify in several directions from Stroud valley. Though, for reasons stated in a previous memoir,* the sands which lie between the Upper Lias clay and Inferior Oolite are considered liassic, yet it is proper to observe, that Mr. Lycett and some other geologists view these beds as composing an independent zone.

Upper Lias Clay.—This forms a thin band of blue clay in Stroud and Nailsworth valleys, and is marked g^8. It is rarely exposed to view, but its presence is indicated by the outburst of springs and marshy ground. The characteristic fossils are—

CHARACTERISTIC FOSSILS OF THE UPPER LIAS CLAY, g^3.

Ammonites opalinus. Rein.
„ serpentinus. Sow.
„ bifrons. Brug.
„ normanianus. D'Orb.
„ thouarcensis. D'Orb.
„ annulatus. Sow.
„ communis. Sow.
„ radians. Schloth.
„ striatalus. Sow.
„ concavus. Sow.
Belemnites elongatus. Miller.
„ compressus. Voltz.
„ irrgularis. Schloth.

Pisces.

Leptolepis concentricus. Ag.

Upper Lias Sand.—This upper member, numbered g^4, consists of fine siliceous sand, with occasional lenticular nodular bands of siliceous limestone, terminated upwards by a bed of calcareo-ferruginous sandstone, frequently well stored with fossils.

This top bed, from the fact of its containing a large number of cephalopoda of liassic species, has been named by Dr. Wright the "cephalopoda bed,"† but together with these there is a con-

* Geology of Cheltenham, by E. Hull.—Memoirs of the Geological Survey, p. 25 et seq.
† Dr. Wright, Quart. Jour. Geol. Soc., Nov. 1856.

siderable number of other mollusca, some of which connect the formation with the Inferior Oolite. Near their junction with the clay the sands become very argillaceous, showing a passage in mineral character, while they also contain several characteristic fossils in common with the Upper Lias clay.

Sections may be seen at Toadmoor Mills, Baker Mill Brimscomb, and in many of the lanes about Nailsworth and Rodborough.

FOSSILS FROM THE UPPER LIAS SAND, STROUD VALLEY, g^4.

Ammonites opalinus. Reineke.
„ bifrons. Brug.
„ radians. D'Orb.
„ Jurensis. Zieten.
„ concavus. Sow.
„ variabilis. D'Orb.
„ communis. Sow.
„ raquinianus. D'Orb.
Belemnites compressus. Voltz.
„ irregularis. Schloth.
Chemnitzia lineata. Sow.
Lima ornata. Sow.
Pecten textorius. Goldf.
Arca inæquivalvis. Goldf.
Turbo capitaneus Münst. Münst.
Pholadomya fidicula. Sow.
Modiola plicata. Sow.
Hinnites abjectus. Phill.
Gresslya adducta. Phill.
Myoconcha crassa. Sow.
Astarte rugulosa. Lyc.
Terebratula sub-punctata. David.
Rhynchonella cynocephala. Richard.
„ furcillata. Theodore.

OOLITES.

LOWER OOLITES.

Inferior Oolite.—This formation, marked g^5, introduces the Oolitic series, named from the oolitic or egg-like form of the grains of some of its limestones. The thickness of the Inferior Oolite at Stroud is about 150 feet, or 110 feet less than at Leckhampton Hill, near Cheltenham. The principal sections occur at Nailsworth in quarries, and natural cliffs at Brimscomb, and in the deep cuttings of the Great Western Railway in the Golden Valley. The Inferior Oolite frequently forms tabulated spurs bounded by abrupt banks which are planted with beech trees and pines; of such there are good examples in Slaughterford Valley.

The following subdivisions may be observed in this district, and can be distinguished both by lithological and fossil characters :—

Inferior Oolite. Rodborough Common.

	Feet.
Upper ragstone. (Clypeus grit.) Coarse rubbly white oolite, with *Terebratula globata, Clypeus, Serpula* - - -	15
Lower ragstone. Shelly limestone, rather sandy, and irregularly bedded, with casts of *Trigonia costata, Gryphæa Buckmani* -	25
Upper freestone. Compact oolitic freestone, quarried for building purposes - - - - - - - -	15
Oolite marl. Cream-coloured marl and chalky limestone, characterized by *Terebratula fimbria* - - - -	5
Lower freestone. Massive, fine grained oolite, false bedded; becoming coarser and somewhat sandy towards the base; quarried for building - - - - - - - -	30
	90

No. 1.

Section at Wall's Quarry, North of Minchinhampton.

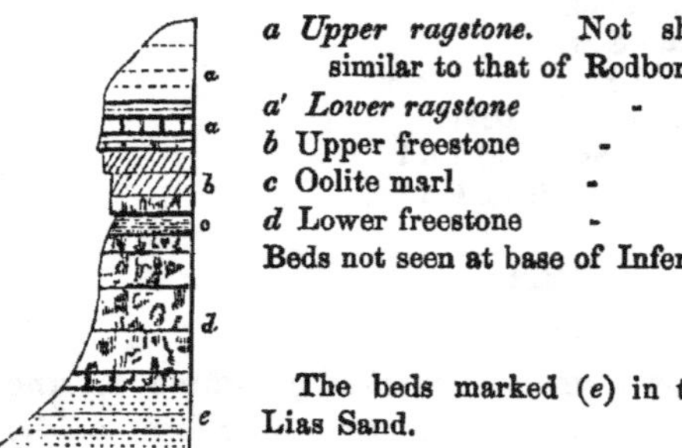

a Upper ragstone. Not shown in section, similar to that of Rodborough Common -	12?
a' Lower ragstone - - - -	9
b Upper freestone - - - -	10
c Oolite marl - - - -	3
d Lower freestone - - - -	15
Beds not seen at base of Inferior Oolite -	10
	59

The beds marked (*e*) in the woodcut are Upper Lias Sand.

From a comparison of these sections it will be observed that the formation has lost some of its thickness in the distance from Rodborough Common to Wall's Quarry. This fact is in harmony with the observed attenuation of the Inferior Oolite, both towards the east and south from Leckhampton Hill, the typical section of this formation.*

The fossils of this formation are so numerous that it is only necessary to mention here a few of the more typical.

FOSSILS FROM THE INFERIOR OOLITE, g^5.

Ammonites Murchisoniæ. Sow.	Astarte excavata. Sow.
„ concavus. Sow.	„ elegans. Sow.
„ Parkinsoni. Sow.	Trigonia striata. Sow.
„ falcifer. Sow.	„ costata. Park.
„ subradiatus. Sow.	Gervilia Hartmani. Goldf.
Nautilus truncatus. Sow.	Ceromya concentrica. Sow.
„ lineatus. Sow.	Myoconcha crassa. Sow.
„ obesus. Sow.	Pecten lens. Sow.
Belemnites abbreviatus. Miller.	Lima gibbosa. Sow.
„ elongatus. Miller.	„ proboscidea. Sow.
„ sulcatus. Miller.	Pinna cuneata. Sow.
Pleurotomaria punctata. Sow.	Avicula complicata. Buck.
„ ornata. Def.	Gryphæa Buckmani. Mor.
„ elongata. Sow.	Ostræa Marshii. Sow.
and casts of many other species.	„ gregaria. Sow.
Cirrus nodosus. Sow.	Terebratula perovalis. Sow.
Chemnitzia lineata. Sow.	„ globata. Sow.
„ ornata.	„ Buckmani. Dav.
Natica casts.	„ fimbria. Sow.
Nerinæa casts.	Rhynconella sub-tetrahedra. Davis.
Myacites dilatatus. Buck.	„ spinosa. Schloth.
„ Jurassi. Brong.	Hyboclypus agariciformis. Forbes.
Greslya abducta. Phil.	Holectypus depressus. Lam.
Cucullæa oblonga. Sow.	Hemipedina Bakeri. Wright.
Pholadomya fidicula. Sow.	Nucleolites clunicularis. Llhwyd.
„ ambigua. Sow.	Pygaster semisulcatus. Phill.
Modiola gibbosa. Sow.	Echinus germinans.
„ Jurensis. Bronn.	Serpula socialis. Goldf.

Fuller's Earth.—This is a stratum of clay with occasional bands of limestone, altogether about 60 feet thick, marked g^6. It forms the base of the Great Oolite. Sections are very rare, as at the outcrop it is generally covered by detritus of Great

* Compare the Maps of the Geological Survey 44 and 35. Also Memoir on the Geology of Cheltenham, pp. 31—47.

Oolite, and it is not now sought after for fulling purposes. Its position is indicated by springs, marshes, and moist ground. In a lane east of the village of Slaughterford we get the following sections:—

	Feet.
1. White marls with occasional stony bands - - - - -	25
2. White and grey limestone and marlstone (Fuller's earth rock) -	10
3. White and blue calcareous clays with *Terebratula perovalis* and *T. maxillata* - - - - - - - - - - .	30
	65

FOSSILS FROM THE FULLER'S EARTH, g^6.

Pholadomya lyrata. Sow.
Modiola gibbosa. Sow.
„ Hillana. Sow.
Goniomya angulifera. Sow.
Lima duplicata. Sow.
Ostrea accuminata. Sow.
Ostrea gregaria. Sow.
Avicula echinata. Sow.
Rhynconella concinna. Sow.
„ media. Sow.
Acrosalenia spinosa. Agsas.

Great Oolite.—This formation, marked g^7, is capable of being divided into two well-marked zones or stages—similar to those which have been shown to exist in the neighbourhood of Cheltenham, and extending eastward into Oxfordshire*:—the lower zone, which comprises the Stonesfield slate; and the upper, of which the typical section occurs in this sheet at Sapperton Tunnel.

Lower zone. At the base of the Great Oolite, along the margins of Stroud and Nailsworth valleys, a few inches or feet of brown sandy slates with partings of clay may frequently be observed, which probably represents the Stonesfield slate of Eyeford and Sevenhampton, although the characteristic fossil *Trigonia impressa* is wanting. This is surmounted by from 20 to 40 feet of white shelly oolite, in which false bedding is prevalent, being, indeed, a characteristic feature of this zone. The fossils are very abundant, as has been shown by Mr. Lycett, but they are generally in a fragmentary state, and give evidence of having been drifted by currents.

* See Memoirs of the Geological Survey,—Geology of Cheltenham p. 53, et seq.

These beds furnish the valuable "Bath freestone," which near Corsham is worked underneath the Forest marble by means of vertical shafts and tunnel work. One of these at Lower Pickwick is 70 feet in depth, and the stone when brought to the surface is easily cut by the saw. Quarries have also been opened in Minchinhampton Common, Brisley Common, and Oakridge Common, at the north-east side of which, and at Battlescomb, the basement beds have been worked for roofing purposes; and further to the east, at Baunton near Cirencester, the same false-bedded shelly oolites are exposed to view in a quarry west of the turnpike road.

The *upper zone* consists of limestone of a blue colour, but weathering white on exposure, in regular massive beds, and is admirably exhibited in the deep cuttings on each side of the smaller tunnel at Sapperton, on the Great Western Railway, where it is 30 feet thick, dipping S.E. at 2°.

The main feature by which it may be distinguished from the lower zone on the one hand, and the Forest marble on the other, is the regularity of the bedding, and the more perfect character of the fossils. Over an area of at least 60 miles in length (already mapped by the Survey), from Banbury to Corsham, and northwards to the borders of the Cotteswold range, this upper zone everywhere presents the character of an evenly-bedded *white limestone*, and is generally so hard as to be eagerly sought for, in preference to any other rocks of the neighbourhood, as road material. The absence of false bedding, and the usually perfect state of the fossils as contrasted with those of the lower zone and of the Forest marble, are features of importance, not to be disregarded when treating of the subdivisions of the Oolites. They show that physical changes had intervened, producing over these regions, in the present case, a sea of a tranquil character; and that, during the deposition of the earlier and later stages of the Great Oolite, the sediments were influenced by marine currents, and other causes that produce irregular stratification or false bedding.

The junction of these zones is generally well defined, and can be observed in a quarry at Yatton Kennel near Corsham, in which we find the following section.

No. 2.

Quarry at Yatton Kennel.

a (*Forest marble*). Fissile shelly oolite, resting obliquely on the Great Oolite, 4 feet.

b *Great Oolite* (*upper zone*). Regularly bedded massive shelly limestone, 7 feet.

c (*Lower zone.*) Shelly oolite, full of false bedding. The upper part coarse; the lower affording very fine building stone, which is followed underground, 16 feet.

The superposition of the two zones is also open to view in a road-cutting on the east side of Castle Combe.

Besides the sections already mentioned, we may notice the following:—quarry east of Tetbury; road section, Thames Head Bridge, south-west of Cirencester; quarries south of Bisley; quarry on the Cheltenham Road, one mile from Stratton; also road-cutting at Stratton; quarry near the railway station, Cirencester; quarry on the Burford road, two miles from Barnsley, on the top of a ridge produced by a fault; quarry north-east of Bibury, and east of Coln St. Aldwin's.

Forest Marble.—All the strata between the white limestone and Cornbrash have been mapped as Forest marble, marked g^8; the white limestone forming a constant and easily recognized base upon which the variable strata of the Forest marble have been deposited. This formation includes shelly fissile oolite, in which false bedding is exceedingly prevalent, together with flagstones, sandy slates, clays, and siliceous sands.

On comparing the eastern portion of the district occupied by Forest marble with the western, it would appear that the fissile oolite of the one occupy the position of the clays and flags of the other. Thus, along the Great Western Railway, the fissile oolite rests on the white limestone, and is succeeded by bluish clays and limestones, shown in the cutting south of Kemble, while on the other hand, east of Cirencester, we find clays and flags resting on the white limestone, and succeeded by fissile oolite, upon which rests the Cornbrash. This will be apparent on comparing the position of the beds in the quarries at Amney with those shown in the Roman road three miles east of Cirencester. Thus we have the clays of one district occupying the position of oolite in another, and vice versâ.

Some of the bluish flagstones of the Forest marble present a curious collection of fragmentary fossils, in which we find shells of *Mollusca*, plates and spines of *Echini*, stems of *Pentacrini*, and fragments of plants strewn over the surface of the slab. Strata of this kind will be found in the quarries at Bicker's Barn and West Yatton near Corsham, the Folly north of Tetbury, in the quarries around Shipton Moyne, at Dudley House near Amney, and in quarries at Barnsley. The finest sections of this formation are exhibited in the railway cuttings at Corsham and Kemble.

In the neighbourhood of Tetbury and Cirencester, we find beds of yellow siliceous sand, containing large blocks of chert, a hard siliceous limestone which, on being split, seldom shows the concretionary structure. These masses may be seen in a quarry near Sandy Lane, south of Cirencester, of which the following is a sketch.

No. 3.

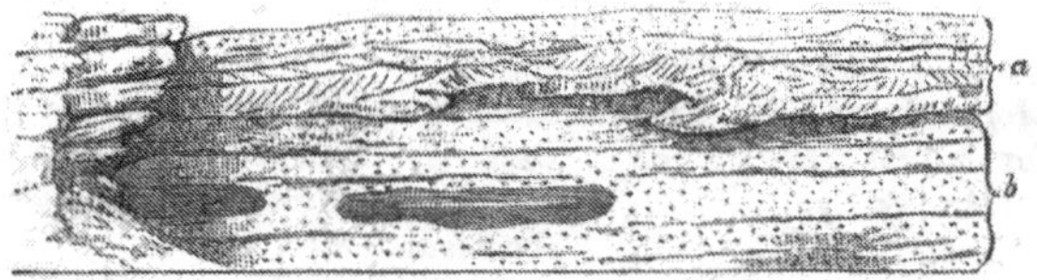

Forest Marble near Cirencester.

a Slaty, false-bedded oolite, with oysters.
b Soft yellow sands, with large blocks of chert.

This bed of sand occurs also at Chavenage Green, north of Beverstone, and at Hillsome near Tetbury. The entire thickness of the Forest marble around Tetbury is about 60 feet, which becomes diminished to more than one half towards the north-east extremity of the district.

FOSSILS FORM THE GREAT OOLITE AND FOREST MARBLE, 9[7], 9[8].

Zoophyta.

Anabacia orbulites. Lam.
Cladophyllia Babeana. D'Orb.
Cyathophora Prattii. M. Edw.
Eunomia radiata. Lam.
Isastrea explanulata. McCoy.
„ limitata. Lam.
Microsolena excelsa. M. Edw.
Thamnastrea concinna. Goldf.

Echinodermata.

Nucleolites Wrightii.
Acrosalenia hemicidaroides. Wright.
„ spinosa. Ag.
Nucleolites clunicularis. Llhwyd.
Nucleolites orbicularis.
„ soludurinus. Ag.
„ sinuatus. Aust.

Brachiopoda.

Terebratula maxillata. Sow.
Rhynconella farcta. Lin.

Gasteropoda.

Pleurotomaria scalaris. Deslong.
Delphinula alta. Morris & Lycett.
Nerita hemispherica. Rœm.
„ rugosa. Mor. & Lyc.
„ cancellata. Mor. & Lyc.
Neritopsis striata. Mor. & Lyc.
Purpuroidea glabra. Mor. & Lyc.
„ nodulata. Mor. & Lyc.
Natica Sharpei. Mor. & Lyc.
„ Verneuili. Arch.
„ Michelini. Arch.
„ pyramidata. Mor. & Lyc.
Phasianella elegans. Mor. & Lyc.
Phasianella Leymeriei. Arch.
Chemnitzia Lonsdalei. Mor. & Lyc.
„ Wetherelli. Mor. & Lyc.
„ Hamptonensis. Mor. & Lyc.
Nerinæa funiculus. Desl.
„ punctata. Voltz.
„ Voltzii. Desl.
„ Dufresnoyi. Arch.
Alaria paradoxa. Desl.
„ armata. Mor. & Lyc.
„ hamus. Desl.
„ trifida. Phil.

Gasteropoda.

Ceritella conica. Mor. & Lyc.
„ acuta. Mor. & Lyc.
„ unilineata. Mor. & Lyc.
Acteonina parvula. Low.
Patella Aubentonensis. Arch.
„ arachnoidea. Mor. & Lyc.
„ Rœmeri. Mor. & Lyc.
„ rugosa. Sow.
„ cingulata. Goldf.
„ suprajurensis. Bron.
Rimula clathrata. Sow.
Trochus squamiger. Mor. & Lyc.
„ Dunkeri. Mor. & Lyc.
„ Bunburyi. Mor. & Lyc.
„ Ibbetsoni. Mor. & Lyc.
Monodonta Lyellii. Arch.
„ formosa. Mor. & Lyc.
„ Labadyei. Mor. & Lyc.
Solarium disculum. Lyc. & Mor.
Trochotoma obtusa. Mor. & Lyc.
„ discoidea. Rœm.

Conchifera.

Pecten clathratus. Rœm.
„ retiferus. Lyc. & Mor.
„ annulatus. Sow.
„ lens. Sow.
„ vagans. Sow.
Placunopsis Jurensis. Rœm.
Ostræa acuminata. Sow.
„ Sowerbii. Morris.
Hinnites velatus. Goldf.
Trigonia flecta. Lyc. & Mor.
„ Moretoni. Lyc & Mor.
Arca minuta. Sow.
„ æmula. Phil.
„ Prattii. Mor. & Lyc.
Opis lunulatus. Sow.
„ similis. Desh.
Unicardium impressum. Lyc. & Mor.
Pinna ampla. Sow.
Trichites nodosus. Lycett.
Myoconcha crassa. Sow.
Mytilus sublævis. Sow.
Modiola tenuistriatus. Goldf.
„ „ furcatus (*a*). Goldf.
„ „ Binfieldi. Lyc. & Mor.
„ imbricata. Sow.
Lima semicircularis. Mor. & Lyc.
„ duplicata. Sow.
„ ovalis. Sow.
„ Luciensis. D'Orb.
„ cardiiformis. Lyc. & Mor.
Lima impressa. Lyc. & Mor.
Perna Bathonica.
Pteroperna costatula. Lyc. & Mor.
„ pygmea. Dunker.
Gervillia monotis. Deslong.
Avicula echinata. Sow.
Corbula curtansata. Phil.
„ minuta.
Capsa oblita.
„ truncata.
„ n. sp.
Venus nana.
„ isocardioides.
Cypricardia Bathonica. D'Orb.
„ rostrata. Sow.
„ nuculiformis. Rœmer.
Lucina crassa. Sow.
„ Bellona. D'Orb.
Cardium pes.-bovis. D'Arch.
„ Stricklandi. Lyc. & Mor.
Pachyrisma grande. Lyc. & Mor.
Macrodon Hirsonensis. Lyc. & Mor
Cucullæa Goldfussii. Rœm.
„ concinna. Phil.
Trigonia Goldfussii. Rœmer.
„ costata. Park.
„ subglobosa. Lyc. & Mor.
Pholadomya ambigua. Sow.
„ Murchisoniæ. Sow.
„ donacina. Lycett.
Ceromya similis. Mor. & Lyc.
Astarte quadrata, Lyc. & Mor.
„ lurida. Sow.

Cornbrash.—This formation, marked g^9, is remarkably constant in mineral character and in the specific identity of its fossil remains. Although but a thin stratum, varying from 5 to 20 feet, it is one of the most persistent of all the members of the great Oolite. It may be described as a rubbly limestone, of a cream colour when near the surface, but bluish beyond the influence of the atmosphere, as may be seen in the quarries near Rodborne, south of Malmesbury. In some places it contains bands of marl and clay, as at Biddestone, near Corsham, where there are two distinct rock beds, separated by an intercalated bed of clay.

No. 4.

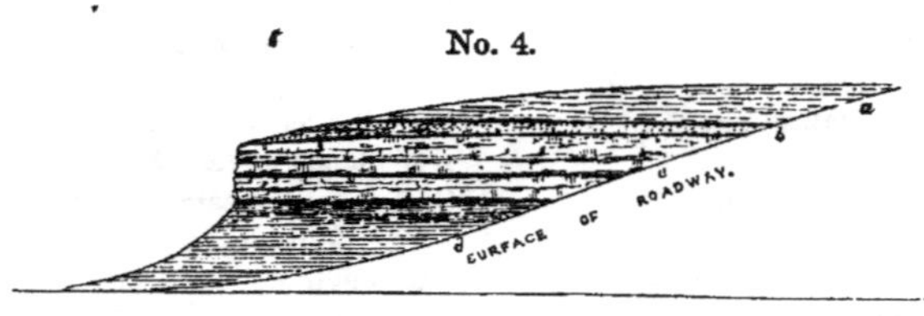

Section in road East of Malmesbury.

a Oxford Clay. Dark blue clay.
b Kelloway Rock. Brown sands and calcareous grits, 2 ft.
c Cornbrash. Blueish thin-bedded fossiliferous limestone, 6 ft.
d Forest Marble. Clays and sandy shales.

The Cornbrash is throughout rich in fossils, which are generally well preserved, and have evidently been entombed in the bed of a tranquil sea.

Sections may be observed in the railway cuttings at Corsham, and in a quarry 100 yards north of the Bath turnpike road, three miles from Chippenham, where I found a specimen of *Pygaster Morrisii.* Quarries and road sections occur at Malmesbury, and particularly at Charlton. There is a road section at Pool Keynes, and quarries by the Ermine Road, south of Cirencester, and another by the Lechlade Road, on the east side of Fairford.

TYPICAL FOSSILS FROM THE CORNBRASH, *g*[9].

Ammonites macrocephalus. Schloth.
„ discus. Sow.
Nautilus lineatus. Sow.
Ostrea gregaria. Sow.
„ acuminata. Sow.
Pecten vagans. Sow.
„ demissus. Phill.
Lima duplicata. Sow.
Avicula echinata. Sow.
Pinna ampla. Sow.
Gervillia acuta. Sow.
Myacites gibbosa. Sow.
Pholadomya Murchisoniæ. Sow.
Goniomya litterata. Goldf.
Unicardium varicosum. Sow.
Astarte rotunda. Sow.
Isocardia minima. Sow.
Ceromya concentrica. Sow.
Terebratula intermedia. Sow.
„ obovata. Sow.
„ lagenalis. Schloth.
Rhynconella concinna. Sow.
„ farcta. Linn.
Pygurus pentagonalis. Phill.
Nucleolites clunicularis. Llhwyd.
„ scutatus. Gmel.
Acrosalenia spinosa. Ag.
Pygaster Morrissii. Wright.

ZOOPHYTES FROM FAIRFORD.*

(Collected by Miss Slatter and J. Jones, Esq.)

Isastrea explanata. Goldf.
„ limitata. Lam.
Thecosmilia annularis. Flenig.
Thamnastrea arachnoides. Park.
Convexastrea Waltoni. M'Edw.
Cladophyllia Conybeari. M'Edw.
Cyathophora Prattii. M'Edw.

MIDDLE OOLITE.

Oxford Clay.—This formation, marked g^{10}, consists of blue clay, attaining a thickness of from 500 to 600 feet. At its base, south of Cirencester, there occurs a thin series of yellowish sands and calcareous sandstone, highly fossiliferous, many of the fossils being those of the Oxford clay. A trace of this rock also occurs at Tetbury (see woodcut No. 4). This bed is known as Kelloway rock.† The great mass of the formation consists of stiff blue clay, which effervesces strongly with acids, weathers pale yellow, and contains frequent bands of septaria. Near its junction with the Cornbrash it generally forms a ridge, which, as at Malmesbury, is frequently capped by flint-gravel. A similar kind of gravel also occurs on the hills of Buscot Park, Garsden, and Flintham.

South of Chippenham the Oxford clay is remarkably narrow, covering an area of only a mile in width, while its breadth at Cricklade is about six miles. Whether this arises from an overlap of the Coral rag, or a local thinning out of the beds is uncertain.

There are but few sections in this formation, as the ground is generally covered with high- or low- level gravels, and the clay is seldom used for bricks or tiles. Sections may be seen in the canal, Chippenham; in a quarry near Bancomb Wood, south of Rodborne at its junction with the Cornbrash; in roads and brick-yards round Malmesbury; in the canal, south of Cirencester; in a brick-yard, east of Minety Station; and in many cuttings of the Great Western Railway. The following section is from Mr. Lonsdale's Memoir on the Geology of Bath:‡—

* These specimens are in the Museum of Practical Geology.

† I believe some Kelloway Rock fossils have been found in these beds, as *Ammonites Callovicensis*, *A. Macrocephalus*, but only local residents have an opportunity of collecting them.—E. H.

‡ Trans. Geol. Soc. vol. iii. p. 260.

No.		Ft.
1.	Pale lead-coloured clay (Oxford clay) - - - -	
2.	Rotten rubbly stone, highly charged with oxide of iron, and inclosing few organic remains - - - - -	5
3.	Sandstone, abounding with fossils - - - -	3
4.	Sand - - - - - - - - -	4
5.	Clay - - - - - -	

TYPICAL FOSSILS FROM THE OXFORD CLAY, g^{10}.

Leptolepis macropthalmus. Egerton.
Aspidorhynchus euodus. Eger.
Ammonites athletus. Phil.
„ macrocephalus. Scloth.
„ Duncani. Sow.
„ Jason. Rein.
„ Gulielmi. Sow.
„ modiolaris. Luid.
Nautilus hexagonus. Sow.
Belemnites Oweni. Pratt.
Pleurotomaria reticulata. Sow.
Rostellaria „
Gryphæa dilatata. Sow.
Ostrea deltoidea. Sow.
„ Marshii. Sow.
„ gregaria. Sow.
Avicula inequivalvis. Sow.
Perna mytiloides. Lam.
Modiola bipartita. Sow.
Thracia depressa. Sow.
“ oblata. Sow.
Trigonia clavellata. Park.
Pholadomya deltoidea.

Lower Calcareous Grit.—This is a series of clays, sands, and calcareous sandstones, marked g^{11}, and forms the base of the Coralline Oolite series, running along the bottom of the Coral Rag throughout the district, but is frequently extremely thin.

The finest section occurs at Highworth, where the formation reaches a thickness of about 100 feet. A quarry at the south side of the town gives the following section :—

Lower Calcareous Grit.—Highworth.

No.		Ft.	In.
1.	Blue and brown clay with fragments of *Pecten*, *Ostrea*, and spines of *Cidaris* - - - - -	6	1
2.	Coarse earthy oolite, with badly preserved fossils - -	1	6
3.	Soft sand, made up of oolitic particles, with *Myacites*, *Pecten*	0	10
4.	Hard bluish oolite, weathering grey, with two soft, very fossiliferous bands, in which were observed *Ammonites per-armatus*, *Myacites recurva*, *Pecten arcuatus*, *P. vimineus* (*varius*), *P. annulatus*, *Nucleolites*, and many other fossils in a fragmentary state - - - - -	4	0
5.	Coral bed, soft calcareo-ferruginous sandstone, with numerous *Echini*, corals, and broken *Nerinæa* - - -	0	8
6.	Hard thick calcareous sandstone, with blue centres, and towards the bottom wedge-shaped - - - -	4	10
7.	Soft siliceous white and yellow sand - - - -	6	0

Nos. 4 and 6 are quarried for road material, and good bricks and tiles are made from a mixture of the clay and sand at the top and bottom of the quarry. The dip is south-east at 1°. Another good section may be observed in the Lechlade road, north of Farringdon, where the thickness of the beds is about 60 feet. At Grittenham Hill the formation is about 50 feet thick, composed principally of yellow sand and thin false-bedded fissile sandstone, capped by a bed of Coral Rag, which may be seen in a small quarry. On the whole this formation is very variable in thickness, and in some places, as at Clack and north of Wootton Basset, appears to be absent. The fossils are nearly identical with those of the Coral Rag, of which it is a subordinate member.

FOSSILS FROM THE LOWER CALCAREOUS GRIT, g^{11}.

Ammonites triplex.	Sow.	Highworth.
„ cordatus.	„	„
„ biplex.	„	„
„ sublævis.	„	Studley.
„ per-armatus	„	„
Belemnites abbreviatus.	Miller.	Highworth.
Natica.		
Pleurotomaria reticulata.	Sow.	„
Chemnitzia Heddingtonensis.	„	„
Cucullæa oblonga.	„	„
Pholadomya Murchisoniæ.	„	„
Gryphæa dilatata.	„	„
Pecten arcuatus.	„	„
Ostrea gregaria.	„	„
Nucleolites scutatus.	Gmel.	„
Isastrea oblonga.	Flem.	„

Coral Rag or *Coralline Oolite*, g^{11}.—This remarkable series consists of beds of rubbly oolite, alternating with coral zones, which are more or less inconstant. The corals are frequently imbedded in an earthy matrix, and the stratification is usually indistinct. Next to the corals the most characteristic fossils are *Echini*, the spines and plates of the *Cidaridæ* forming a frequent feature in hand specimens.

The thickness of this formation varies from fifteen to twenty-five feet, and at its northern outcrop produces a ridge of from 100 to 200 feet above the plain of the Oxford Clay.

As the Coral Rag is largely quarried for road material, sections are numerous along its course from Calne to Farringdon. The following are the most important:—Quarries around Calne, at Whitley Farm, Wootton Basset; in quarries and railway cuttings at Purton, Grittenham Hill, between Lyneham and Fastern Farm, and in many sections around Farringdon.

Upper Calcareous Grit.—This is a local deposit of ferruginous sand, occurring only at intervals, marked g^{11}. There are no good sections, but it has been cut through by the canal south of Shrivenham, and its presence is generally indicated by the bright red colour of the ground. The localities where it occurs in the district are Shrivenham and Lyneham, and at both places it is separated from the Coral Rag by a parting of clay.

FOSSILS FROM THE CORAL RAG, *g*.

Species	Authority	Locality
Cidaris Blumenbachii.	Munst.	Hillmarton.
„ Florigemma.	Phill.	Purton.
Diadema subangulare.	Goldf.	Hillmarton.
Diadema pseudo-diadema.	Lam.	„
Acroselenia hemicidaroides.	Wright.	„
Glypticus hieroglyphicus.		„
Nucleolites scutatus.	Sow.	„
Ostrea deltoidea.	„	Purton.
„ gregaria	„	„
„ sandalina	„	„
Pecten fibrosus	„	Hillmarton.
Lima rigida	„	„
„ proboscidea	„	Purton.
Perna mytiloides	Lam.	Hillmarton.
Gryphæa dilatata	Sow.	„
Lithodomus inclusus.	Phill.	„
Isocardia minima.	Sow.	Purton.
Chemnitzia Heddingtonensis.	Sow.	„
„ lineata	„	„
Littorina muricata	„	„
„ ornata ?	„	„
Pleurotomaria reticulata	„	„
Terebratula ornothocephala	„	„

Corals.

Thecosmilia annularis. Flem.
Cladophyllia Conybeari. M.-Edw.
Thamnastræa arachnoides. Park.
„ concinna. Goldf.
Isastræa Greenoughii. M.-Edw.
„ explanata. Goldf.
Stylina De la Bechii. M.-Edw.
„ tubulifera. Phill.
Comoseris irradians. M.-Edw.

Upper Oolite.

Kimmeridge Clay.—This deposit, marked g^{12}, extends continuously in this Sheet, from Calne to Farringdon, at which places it is completely overlapped by the Lower Greensand, while its greatest breadth is in the neighbourhood of Swindon. It consists of alternating beds of bituminous shales and more compact masses of dark blue clay. Towards the top, nodules of argillaceous limestone occur in layers, as well as sandy marlstone with *Ammonites biplex*, in which the nacreous lustre is well preserved. *Ostrea deltoidea* is common in all the beds. There are no natural sections, but the strata may be observed in brickyards at Swindon, and in the North Wilts canal at Ridgeway, and south of Shrivenham.

Fossils from the Kimmeridge Clay, g^{12}.

Vertebræ of ichthyosaurus and plesiosaurus.
Remains of Pliosaurus.
Asteracanthus ornatissimus. Ag.
Lepidotus Fittoni. Ag.
Hybodus.
Ammonites biplex. Sow.
„ plicatilis. Sow.
Belemnites abbreviatus. Miller.
Littorina muricata. Sow.
Chemnitzia Heddingtonensis. Sow.
Pleurotomaria reticulata. Sow.
Pholadomya æqualis. Sow.
Myacites recurva. Phil.
Cardium striatulum. Sow.
Isocardia minima. Sow.
Astarte lineata. Sow.
„ Hartwellensis. Sow.
Exogyra nana. Sow.
Thracia depressa. Sow.
Ostrea deltoidea. Sow.
Trigonia clavellata. Park.
Gryphæa virgula.
„ deltoidea.
Rhynconella inconstans. Sow.
Discina Humphresiana. „
Serpula.

Portland Oolite and Sand, marked g^{13}, and Purbeck Limestone, g^{14}.—This formation occurs in two detached portions at Swindon and Bourton. At the latter place the Portland beds stand apart as an outlier on the Kimmeridge

Clay between the Lower Greensand and the Great Western Railway.

The Portland beds of Swindon rise from beneath the Lower Greensand by the reservoir in the manner shown in the following diagram (Fig. 5):—

No. 5.

Section from Swindon to Liddington Castle.

a Kimmeridge clay. b Portland sand. c Portland oolite. d Purbeck limestone. e Lower Greensand. f Gault. g Upper Greensand. h Soft chalk. i Hard chalk. k Outlier of Plastic clay.

From the mode of their appearance it is probable that they also may form an outlier the south-east end of which is overlapped by the Lower Greensand, as shown in the middle of the diagram, the uppermost oolitic strata in this area having been subjected to so much denudation before and during the deposition of the Lower Cretaceous beds, that only occasional patches were left, and these of a nature that seems to indicate that the beds were deposited near the original shore margin of the formation.

In the typical district of Portland Bill the section consists of about 150 feet of yellow and bluish grey sands, becoming more clayey as they pass downwards into the Kimmeridge clay. These are overlaid by from 70 to 110 feet of bituminous limestone, occasionally oolitic, and containing masses and bands of chert. But at Swindon the section is less definite; for though it mainly consists of a sandy base overlaid by limestone, yet occasional limestones seem to be intercalated with the sand and calcareous sandstone. One of these occurs on the east bank of the reservoir, where it has been quarried; and there is another mass of limestone shown in a quarry north of the road near Coate, which, judging by the small thickness of the underlying sand, seems to be on a lower stratigraphical horizon than the Portland limestone by the town. It is, however, overlaid in pot holes by traces of the Lower Greensand, and may possibly be the representative of the Portland Limestone itself. It contains the following fossils:—*Ammonites biplex*, *Trigonia gibbosa*, *T. incurva* and an undescribed clavellated species, *Modiola*, *Panopœa*, *Pecten lamellosus*, *Cardium dissimile*, *Lima rustica*, and *Isocardia*.

In the large quarries at Swindon the section in ascending order consists of Portland Sand, Portland Limestone, Purbeck Limestone, and a small thin outlier of Lower Greensand. The rocks are quarried partly for the limestone, but chiefly for blocks and slabs of a calcareous sandstone, which is included in the softer sands in irregular lenticular bands. About a third of the limestone has been already quarried, and if the works continue as vigorously as at present, the whole of the Portland and Purbeck beds of this outlier will, at no distant date, be entirely removed. The section varies so rapidly in different parts of the quarry that, as the works proceed, any details now given may probably not apply to the section as it may exist in a few years.

At the north-east part of the quarry, next the town, the section, about 30 feet thick, described in ascending order, is as follows:—

No. 6.

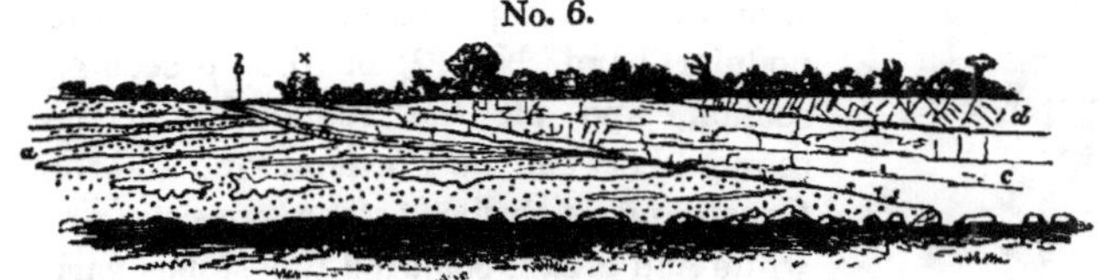

Section at Swindon.

(*a*) *Portland Sand.*—Soft yellowish brown sand with irregular bands and ragged-edged masses of hard calcareous sandstone containing vertical annelide tubes, and casts and burrows of *Lithodomi*, together with a few remains of *Trigonia incurva* and an elongated variety of the same, all with the shell preserved.

(*b*) Bluish grey sand, with carbonaceous specks, and overlaid by vegetable fragments.

(*c*) *Portland Limestone.*—Yellow and cream coloured, about 8 feet thick, including two thin bands of clay (marked with black lines below ×) and full of nodular masses rich in casts of shells.

(*d*) *Purbeck Limestone*, about 4 feet, of a pale yellow colour, shivered in angular pieces, containing fragments of shells.

On the north side of the quarry, somewhat further west, there is the following section described in ascending order:—

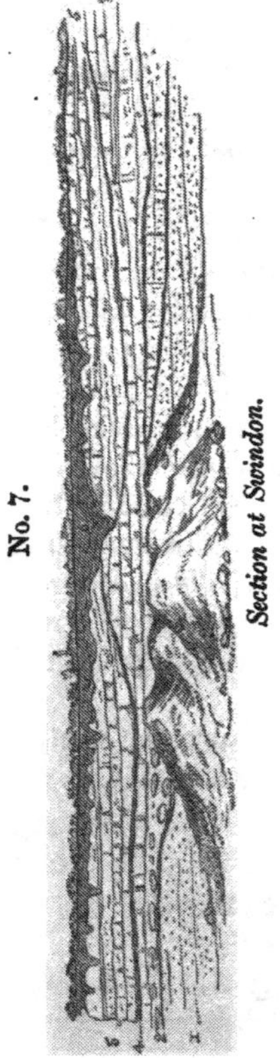

No. 7. *Section at Swindon.*

1. *Portland Sand*, with hard calcareous bands.
2. *Portland Limestone*, consisting of large concretionary or nodular masses of limestone, in a soft calcareous matrix, with numerous casts of *Trigonia gibbosa* and *Terebra Portlandica*, associated with *Cytherea* and *Venus*.
3. Hard cream-coloured limestone from 1 to 6 feet thick, with *Trigonias*, &c.
4. Band of dark sandy clay.
5. *Purbeck Limestone*, consisting of hard pale cream-coloured limestone, with an angular fracture and soft bluish marly limestone. These sometimes alternate, and sometimes in the same beds pass suddenly into each other. They contain *Cyprides?*, and the univalves *Paludina* and *Bithynia*.
6. *Lower Greensand*, ferruginous.

In this quarry the individual beds are so inconstant that a few yards apart the details vary to a considerable extent. Thus at the north-west angle of the quarry, above the sand, the Portland Limestone is represented alone by the nodular band No. 2 of the preceding section, and all the remainder of the section, between the Portland sand and the Greensand, is Purbeck stone, consisting of white and cream-coloured limestones variously intercalated and mingled with soft bluish marly and sandy lime, the whole being interstratified with thin irregular bands of clay. On the west side of the quarry the same kind of beds prevail, the Portland stone being merely represented by very fossiliferous concretions; all the wedge-shaped hard and soft limestones, marly bands, and thin clays above, being undoubted Purbeck beds, yielding, when well searched, casts of *Paludinæ*. At the south-west end of the quarry the Greensand is absent.

The following fossils have been determined by Mr. Etheridge from specimens collected by himself, Mr. Ramsay, and Mr. Richard Gibbs:—

	Sand.	Limestone.
Ostrea expansa. Sow.	—	×
Perna	—	×
Pecten lamellosus. Sow.	—	×
Lucina Portlandica. Sow.	—	×
Modiola	—	×
Panopæa	—	×
Cytherea rugosa. Sow.	—	×
Trigonia gibbosa. Sow.	×	×
" incurva and a long variety like clavellata	×	×
Cardium dissimile. Sow.	×	×
Venus	—	×
Arca, new species	—	×
Gastrochæna	×	×
Terebra Portlandica. Sow.	—	×
Natica	—	×
Pleurotomaria	—	×
Ammonites giganteus. Sow.	—	×
" biplex. Sow.	—	×

The Portland beds of Bourton occupy a small isolated area of half a mile in diameter, forming a hill on which the village is built. The basement bed is composed of yellow sands a few feet thick, above which there occurs a bed of hard fossiliferous limestone, with pebbles of Lydian stone and white quartz; and this again is capped by beds of chalky oolite.

In a large quarry south of the village we find the following section:—

1. Soft thin-bedded chalky oolite, with grains of sand; fossils scarce. 8 feet.

2. Hard bluish limestone, very fossilferous, with *Cardium dissimile*, *Trigonia clavellata*, *T. gibbosa*, *Ostreæ*, *Ammonites giganteus*, *Nucleolites*?

The base of this bed was not seen: it may be considered as representing a shelly bed at the base of the Portland Sands, Swindon, to which subdivision all these beds belong.

Cretaceous.

Lower Cretaceous.

Lower Greensand.—The Lower Greensand is marked *h* 2. There are few places throughout its course in this Sheet where it is well exposed, or its line well defined. Lying in the flats to the west and north of the steep escarpment formed by the Upper Greensand and Chalk, it seldom makes any considerable feature in the country; and to add to the difficulty of tracing its boundaries, it is often covered by detritus from the Chalk. At Cherhill Pen, north-east of Calne, it rises into moderately high ground, forming a hill, the west escarpment of which is Kimmeridge Clay, the top, Lower Greensand, the dip of the beds being of the same amount as that of the eastern slope of the hill.

No. 8.

Section from Cherhill Pen to Highway-field, near Calne.

a Kimmeridge Clay. b Lower Greensand. c Gault.
d Upper Greensand. e Chalk.

At Pinhills, to the south of Calne, an outlier of Lower Greensand caps a hill. Also to the west of Bowood Park it occupies high ground, and in many places along its line a small feature may be detected. Where not too thickly covered by chalk detritus, it may be traced by the redness of the soil; and there are places where the rock itself is exposed, as at Sands Farm, to the east of Calne, on Cherhill Pen, where there are a few openings, and it has also been dug up in Highbury churchyard. Again it is seen at Corton, and also in a brook a little south of that place. So far passing northward, the formation can be pretty accurately traced. At Woodhill Park Farm it is rather obscure, and continues so for some way further to the north-east. Lying, however, between the Kimmeridge Clay and the Gault, both of which make wet ground, while the sand forms a remarkably dry soil, this of itself affords a good indication of the position of the sand, even when no sections are seen, either through the scarcity of openings or a covering of chalk drift.

The general character of the Lower Greensand is a yellow or red ferruginous unconsolidated sand, with irregular bands of ironstone, and balls of clay ironstone decomposing red on the outside. There are, however, a few exceptions, one of these is at Sands Farm, where a part of the formation is composed of a very pure and beautifully fine white quartz sand. It has long been extensively worked, and is carried to great distances for domestic purposes. The white sand is the lowest bed here seen. It is overlaid by yellow sand, and that again by red sand. There are no consolidated beds in the white sand, but in the yellow strata there are lumps of hardened sand, and in the red beds layers of ironstone. In these pits no fossils have yet been found. Sometimes a conglomerate forms the base of the Lower Greensand. Such is the case in a quarry a little to the south of Woodhill Park Farm. On the hill south of Can Court there is an outlier, and in a quarry there, of red and yellow sand, there is a bed of coarse hard grit full of fossils.

The Lower Greensand is very irregular in thickness, changing in this respect within very short distances. Not having any immediate geological connexion with the formations above or below, it is occasionally overlapped by the Gault (as in Sheet 14), and the sand itself overlaps and rests on various formations below. To the west of Bowood Park it lies on the lower beds of the Coral Rag; at Pinhill, partly on that formation and partly on Kimmeridge Clay. At the edge of the Sheet, about a mile south of Calne, the Kimmeridge Clay appears from under it, having in the country further south been overlapped for several miles. From Swindon to Farringdon it generally forms a slightly-elevated feature rising above the Kimmeridge clay. At Swindon it rests on Purbeck and Portland beds; and in the quarries there may be observed occupying pipes and furrows formed in Purbeck and Portland limestone and sand. A similar section is exposed in a quarry on the east bank of the reservoir.

The thickness of the Greensand is here about twenty-five feet, consisting of bright yellow ferruginous sand, sometimes clayey, full of pebbles of hard chert or dark Lydian stone, waterworn and polished. Bands and fragments of silicious iron ore are frequent. At Chappelwick Farm, near Shrivenham, the Lower Greensand has been proved fifteen feet deep at least. It there consists of coarse ferruginous sand of various colours, in which pebbles of the following rocks were observed :—Oolitic limestone (probably from the Portland series), dark Lydian stone, or altered slate in small fragments, and calcareous slate. Sections are also visible at Stainswick Farm, and in the railway cutting at Ruffinswick Farm.

South of Farringdon, this formation suddenly assumes an importance greater than in any other part of Wiltshire, as it contains a remarkable series of fossiliferous beds, known as the Farringdon Gravels. These beds consist of fragmentary *Sponges*, *Bryozoa*, *Echini*, and *Mollusca* more or less waterworn, pebbles of hardened slate or Lydian stone, and white or coloured quartz, the whole being cemented into a conglomerate by ferrugino-calcareous cement.

These gravels appear to occupy an isolated position, and though best exhibited in the neighbouring Sheet they are described in this notice as they extend into Sheet 34, at Little Coxwell. They stretch from the turnpike road north of Little Coxwell to Fernham on the south, and rest immediately on the Kimmeridge clay, being overlaid by soft silicious sands, with beds of chert and iron ore, of which Bradbury Hill, Furze Hill, and Alfred's Hill are composed. The following is the section at Fernham :—

	Feet.
1. Soft yellow sands, with bands of iron ore, containing *Leda scapha*, D'Orb., and *Venus parva* -	40
2. Bed of clay and fuller's earth - - -	10
3. Hard calcareous conglomerate, with *sponges* and *bryozoa* (sponge gravel) - - - -	12
4. Soft yellow, red, and green sands - - -	10
	72

The finest sections of the sponge gravels are shown in two large quarries at Little Coxwell. In the more westerly of these we obtain a total section (measured at right angles to the apparent dip) of 45 feet. In this quarry the greater proportion of the rock is composed of fragmentary *Sponges*, *Bryozoa*, *Echini*, and *Mollusca*, the remainder being formed of small pebbles of quartz, slate, and hornstone, rounded and waterworn. The whole of these constituents are bound into a firm gravel by a calcareo-ferruginous cement. At about the centre there is a lenticular band of sandy limestone. The apparent dip is east-south-east at 6°. The general colour of the gravel is bright yellow, and when crushed is much sought after as a gravel for walks and avenues.

The same beds are again shown in a quarry about a quarter of a mile further towards the east. Here, however, the inorganic elements predominate, and the fossils, consisting of *Sponges*, *Echini*, *Mollusca*, and *Cephalopoda*, are less numerous than in the quarry at Little Coxwell. In both cases, however, they are generally waterworn, broken, and appear to have travelled. The beds in this quarry dip westward, so that the sponge gravels form a synclinal curve, the axis of which runs between the two quarries just described.

At Fernham we again meet these beds in the form of a hard quartzose conglomerate, as already stated, in which the pebbles are frequently an inch in diameter, the fossils are generally in casts.

These sponge gravels are not continuous *along* the outcrop from Little Coxwell to Fernham, but the superimposed sands appear in some places to overlap them along the borders, and rest directly on the Kimmeridge clay.

The beds above the sponge gravels consist of soft yellow sands, with bands of clay, chert, and iron ore. They may be well seen at Badbury Hill, Furze Hill, and Alfred's Hill. The strata of all these places must be regarded as occupying the same general horizon. The bands of iron ore strongly resemble those of Shotover Hill, near Oxford; but whereas those of Shotover Hill contain only freshwater shells, those of Furze Hill are marine.

The unconformity of the Lower Greensand to both the Kimmeridge Clay and Gault, is abundantly manifest within the limits of the district. We find this formation resting on the Coral Rag at Little Coxwell, where it has entirely overlapped the Kimmeridge Clay; while north of Baulking the Gault rests on the Kimmeridge Clay without the intervention of the Lower Greensand.

FOSSILS FROM THE SPONGE GRAVELS OF THE LOWER GREENSAND, FARRINGDON, h^2.†

Brachiopoda.

Rhynconella nuciformis. Sby.
Terebratula menardi. Lanck.
Terebratula nerviensis. D'Ar.
„ tornacensis. Forb.

Conchifera.

Avicula.
Spondyllus.
Exogyra conica. Sow.
Lucina Farringdonensis.*
Dianchora Guttata.*
Plicatula inæquidens.*

Cephalopoda.

Belemnites.
Nautilus Lævigata. D'orb.*

Zoophyta.

Manon Farringdonensis.* Sharpe.
„ Peziza. Goldf.
„ Porcatum.* Sharpe.
Manon macropora.* Sharpe.
Verticillipora anastomosans.* Mantel.
Chenendopora fungiformis.* Lamx.

Echinodermata.

Cidaris coronatus.
Salenia punctata. Ag.
Goniopagus peltatus. Ag.

UPPER CRETACEOUS.

Gault.—The Gault succeeds the Lower Greensand, and is the lowest member of the Upper Cretaceous rocks. It is marked on the map *h* 3. In consequence of its soft nature it forms low ground, and being often covered with drift, there are few places where it is well exposed. In the next Sheet

† All those species marked * are described and figured by Sharpe, Geo. Quart. Journal, vol. x. p. 194, et sup.

For further descriptions of the Farringdon Gravels, and theoretical considerations concerning their origin, see R. A. C. Austen, Quart. Journ. Geol. Soc., Vol. vi., p. 454.

to the south it is often opened for brick making, but when Sheet 34 was mapped there was only one brickyard at work in the Gault, at a spot between Budburywick and Greenhill, south-east of Swindon. The Gault generally consists of a stiff blue clay, full of small spangles of mica, and occasionally it contains calcareous concretions, septaria, and sometimes phosphatic nodules; and though there are few sections exposed, there is every reason to believe that throughout this Sheet it maintains its usual characteristics.

The wet and clayey nature of the soil contrasts both with the dryness of the Lower and Upper Greensands; and the springs thrown out at its top not only afford good indications of its presence, but are guides in tracing its upper boundary.

Upper Greensand.—This formation, marked *h* 4, immediately succeeds the Gault, into which there appears to be a passage. Its thickness at Devizes, in the Sheet below, is 138 feet, but where it enters on the south side of this map it is much thinner, and during its course to the north-east it continues to decrease in thickness. In a well sunk at Odstone Farm, near its top boundary on the east side of the Sheet, 40 feet were gone through with 5 feet of Gault below. Between Cherhill, east of Calne and Wroughton, its upper beds form a steep escarpment or cliff made by landslips. In some places the whole of the formation is contained in this cliff, being capped by the Chalk, and having the Gault at its base. This is the case at Bricknole, east of Wroughton, where it consequently occupies but a very small breadth on the map. From Wroughton to Compton Beauchamp the escarpment is not so steep. In consequence of the slips, the boundary between the Gault and the Upper Greensand is generally completely obscured, and were it not for wells and a few cuttings, it would be altogether uncertain. In a well sunk at Theobald's Green, east of Calne, the junction beds were gone through, which gives the boundary very accurately there. From Theobald's Green to Compton Basset House it is uncertain, but at the latter place both the upper and lower boundaries can be exactly ascertained, the base of the Chalk being seen a little way to the south-east of the house on the slope of the hill, Greensand at the house, and Gault below on the west side. The next place to the north where the junction is visible is in the Highway gully, and at a cottage farther north-east Gault is seen. From this place to Wroughton, with the exception of Bincknoll gully, where there is a good section, the boundary can be only traced by the aid of springs, wells, and the general appearance of the ground. The general form of the ground under the Chalk escarpment is thus:—

No. 9.

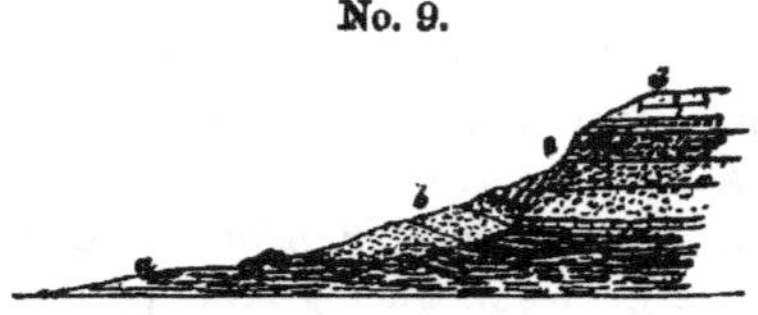

Landslip of Upper Greensand and Clalk.

a Gault. *b* Fallen greensand and chalk. *c* Upper greensand. *d* Chalk.

As the fallen rocks are not marked on these maps, the boundary between the Gault and Upper Greensand must be placed somewhere between the top and bottom of the debris; and if placed half way up, or perhaps a little nearer the top, it would be found to be approximately correct if the fallen rocks were removed. From Wroughton to the eastern side of the Sheet the boundary can only be traced by the aid of wells and springs, and, next to seeing the actual junction, there cannot be better guides to indicate the line. In fact, it is well marked by the villages, built on account of the water, which is everywhere thrown out along the junction.

The general character of the Upper Greensand in this Sheet is a light brown and grey sand, speckled with green grains, and containing occasional hard irregular beds of sandstone and chert. These hard beds die away towards the east. The best sections are at Cherhill, where it is on the top a fine green-grained sand, with a coarser variety at bottom. The same is seen at Compton Bassett. At Highway there is a very good section; here the beds are soft at the top and bottom, with hard sandstone in the middle. At Cliff Pypard light brown or grey sand is seen, but the section is not very good. The same sands are also visible at Broad Town. At Wroughton and Liddington there are pretty fair sections; no hard beds are seen in the latter place, and poor exposures of the strata are also seen at Warborough and Ashbury. At Ashbury it is light in colour, indicating the commencement of a passage into those white beds which are the representatives of the Upper Greensand in Berkshire and Oxfordshire. First, it passes into fine white siliceous strata, which, in their strike further east, pass through various calcareous gradations into absolute chalk, to be subsequently explained in a forthcoming notice of Sheet 13. Though diligently searched, no fossils have been yet found by the survey in the Gault and Upper Greensand of this Sheet.

Chalk.—The Chalk is coloured on the map a pale green, and marked *h* 5. It occupies the chief area (about 96 square miles) of the south-east corner of the Sheet, being only overlaid by a few thin Tertiary outliers.

The boundary between the Upper Greensand and the Chalk is often very obscure, in consequence of slips of the latter over the former; and these, having slid down bodily in great masses, often appear as if they were in their proper position undisturbed. (See Diagram No. 9.) To render the boundary still more uncertain, many of the deep gullies made by the brooks that run off the Chalk, and where a section might be looked for, are full of recomposed chalk, covering the junction beds. The slips occur chiefly between Cherhill and Chisledon. Farther eastward, the boundary is easy to trace.

The Chalk may be separated into two great divisions, a Lower or soft Chalk, and an Upper or hard Chalk.

The Lower Chalk contains very few flints, and is especially soft near the bottom, where it often partakes more of the character of a marl. In many places the surface of the ground is wet and rushy, as in the neighbourhood of Broad Hinton and Winterbourn Basset. The colour is generally milk white, sometimes approaching to a creamy tint.

Wherever the bottom of the Lower Chalk is well exposed there is seen at its base a pale yellowish-coloured marl, with black spots of a chloritic mineral, and full of nodules of iron. Although it seldom exceeds a couple of yards in thickness, it is very constant in this district, and whatever the thickness of the Upper Greensand may be, it invariably separates it from the ordinary Chalk. This being the case, and its marly character partaking more of the marly chalk above than of the sandy formation below, it has been considered as forming the base of the Chalk.

The best places where this chloritic marl is seen are, on the road leading to Oldborough Castle, east of Compton Basset; the road to Highway Field, where the marl contains fossils; and Cleve-ancy, where fossils are also found. A very good junction between the Upper Greensand and this marl is to be seen in the dingle at Bincknoll, south-west of Swindon. From Chisledon to the east side of the Sheet the Chalk marl is to be seen on several of the roads leading from the small villages to the chalk downs. Fossils occur plentifully in the chloritic marl in some places, but not throughout its entire extent.

The characteristic fossils of the Chalk marl are—

	Highway.	Cliff Pypard.	Quiddington
Rynchonella latissima. Sow. - -	—	—	×
„ compressa. Lam. - -	—	—	×
Inoceramus latus. Mant. - - -	—	×	—
Plicatula inflata. Sow. - - -	×	—	×
Pleurotomaria perspectiva. Mant. -	×	—	—
Turrilites tuberculatus. Bosc. - -	—	—	×
Ammonites varians. Sow. - -	—	×	×
„ rothomagensis. Brong. -	—	×	×
Nautilus elegans. Sow. - - -	×	—	—

The following additional species are found almost universally in these beds:—

Terebratula biplicata. Sow.
Ostrea vesicularis. Lane.
Pecten quinquecostata. Sow.
Plicatula pectinoides. Sow.
Mytilus lineatus.
Venericardia tenuicosta. Sow.
Avellana cassis. D'Orb.
Turritella.
Scaphites æqualis. Sow.
Hamites simplex. D'Orb.
Nautilus lævigatus. D'Orb.
Ananchytes subglobosus. Leske.
Galerites castanea. Brog.

The Upper Chalk is hard, and contains innumerable layers of flints. These, being washed out and left exposed where the chalk has been decomposed and carried away in solution, thickly cover the ground not only of the higher hills occupied by the hard Chalk, but they have also been drifted down and spread over the Lower soft Chalk.

The unequal denudation of the hard and soft Chalk forms a striking feature in this part of the country, especially when viewed from the west and north-west. The hard Chalk rising abruptly out of the high and broad plateau of the soft Chalk, the bare grassy sides and tops of the former contrast strongly with the cultivated plains of the latter. And while the plateau of the Lower Chalk rises and falls in gentle undulations, interspersed with small streams, the Upper Chalk is cut up into numerous ridges and valleys, and is nearly destitute of water.

A bay or inlet of the Lower Chalk running by Ogbourn St. George and Ogbourn St. Andrew's towards Marlborough separates into two divisions the high escarpment of the Upper Chalk, that on the west forming Marlborough Downs; the Castle of Barbury Hill on the north side of these downs, and Liddington Castle on the north-west of the other division, forming high and conspicuous objects.

From Liddington to the north-east the contrast between the Upper and Lower Chalk is not so well marked, the hard chalk not being denuded so far back, nor is the rise from the one to the other so abrupt. They unite, indeed, with the Upper Greensand to form one escarpment directly overlooking the plain of Gault and Kimmeridge clay.

Eocene.

Plastic Clay.—This formation lies in patches on the highest ridges of the chalk Downs. It is coloured a dark brown, and marked *i* 2. These outliers are mere remnants of a tertiary formation that once covered the Chalk. They are classed by Mr. Prestwich with the Woolwich and Reading series. He divides the lower part of the Tertiary strata in descending order thus :—

1. Basement beds of the London clay.
2. Woolwich and Reading series.
3. Thanet sands.

The Thanet sands are absent in this part of the country, so that here the lowest Tertiary formation is the Woolwich and Reading series, of which small outlying fragments alone remain; any other formation that may have been above, having been removed by denudation. Mr. Prestwich, in writing of the same formation in Marlborough Forest, which adjoins this sheet on the south, says, "The beds are so thin, and so disturbed by or mixed with drift, that no good section can be obtained. Enough, however, is exposed to see that they consist of mottled clays, with sands and pebble beds reposing on the chalk." The same may be said of the Tertiary clays in this Sheet, and not only do they thinly cover the surface of the Chalk, but also fill hollows and pipes or pot holes in that formation, often to a considerable depth. These, according to Mr. Prestwich, were formed, after the clays were deposited, by the gradual destruction of the underlying chalk by acids contained in the water that sunk through the clays; and as the chalk was dissolved and carried away through the numerous cracks in that formation, the clays and sands above were slowly pressed down by their own weight and filled the hollows thus made. These views seem correct.

The following is a detailed description of the Plastic clays and sands in this Sheet:—Along the top of the ridge which runs from Marlborough in an east-north-east direction to the south of the river Kennett, wherever a pit has been sunk there have been found yellow sand and red or yellow clay, spreading thinly over the surface of the Chalk, or filling pot holes to some depth.

In a pit sunk on the plain to a depth of 20 feet, chalk occupies one side nearly to the surface, while on the other sides are mottled clays and yellow sands to the bottom. There is one place in this ridge where the clay is worked for making bricks, three miles to the east of Marlborough, and here the mottled clays and yellow sands lie in hollows made in a coarser red clay and yellow sand mixed with angular flints.

Clays cover the tops of the hills north-east of Marlborough. Round Hill Copse is full of pits containing red clay mixed with flints. At the brick kiln, on the west side of Round

Hill Copse, there are holes from which yellow sands mixed with red and grey clay have been dug. The surface of the ground is a red clay mixed with angular flints. On the south side of the brick kiln there is a large pit of yellowish brown sandy clay containing both rounded and small angular flints. On the top are some large angular flints. Around Bitham the ground is covered with red clay and angular flints, and close by the house there is some yellow sandy clay. About half a mile to the south of the brick kiln is another deep pit of light yellow sand, mixed with red and light blue clay, giving the whole a mottled appearance. Half a mile to the north-north-west of Dudmore Lodge there have been pottery works and yellow sand is to be seen there. Also in a pond at Dudmore Lodge there are some yellow and red clays, as well as some white clay mixed with white sand. At Upper Upham there are red clays mixed with angular flints, and sometimes a little yellow sand. At Love's barn, south of Aldbourn, there is some yellowish brown clay. There is no clay to be seen near Brick Kiln Cottage, and if there ever were brick pits there the clay must either have been drift or taken from some solitary Eocene pot hole now filled up. At a place half a mile north-west of Love's Barn there is a pit of yellow sandy clay, and at another pit more to the south-west there is a thickness of several yards of yellow sandy clay and red clay, with a few round pebbles. At Kew and near Line's farm there are red clays and yellow sands, and in a pond half a mile further east there is some thickness of clay without flints. Everywhere on this ridge, where an opening has been made, bright red clays or yellow sands have been found.

The Tertiary beds on the ridges east of Aldbourn are like those which have been described; red clays and yellow sands, sometimes separate and sometimes mixed, spreading thinly over the surface, and filling pot holes to some depth. In some spots there are round flint pebbles, as at Peashill copse, but generally the clays and sands are mixed with unwaterworn flints. Near the village of Bayden the clays appear to be more pure than they are in general, that is, without so many flints. On the north-east side of Liddington Castle there is a singular looking conglomerate, composed of large angular flints, small round flints, fragments of ironstone, lumps of chalk, red clay, and yellowish brown sand, mixed confusedly together. The Chalk is to be seen in the pit about 10 feet from the surface.

On the south-south-east side of Liddington Castle there are angular flints mixed with a little red clay and yellow sand. The flints, after being sifted from the sand and clay, are used for road making. At a spot half a mile to the north-west of Aldbourn there is a pit of yellowish brown stratified sand, full of small square fragments of flints, that look, at first sight, like fragments of shells. It is a coarse sand with grains of some black substance intermixed, and also angular flints. On the ridge on the north-east side of Wanborough Plain there are some pot holes filled with flint gravel mixed with red clays. The same kind of deposits occur on Bishopstone Down, and also some similar to that at Liddington Castle.

No Tertiary beds have been seen on the ridge east of Ashdown Park. There are a few uncertain outliers a short distance north-east of Marlborough, as, for instance, at Rabley Copse, where red clay is to be seen on the west side and at the south corner, but this may be drift. On Woodland's ridge a dull red clay occurs in places, but the Chalk is also seen near the top. There is also a pot-hole of red clay at the north-east side of the plantation on Polton Down.

On the Marlborough Downs there are also outliers of clays and sands. At the Brick Kiln, now out of use, on Hackpen, there are yellowish red clays and flints. In like manner at Glory Inn there appear to have been some old brick kilns, but the brick kiln marked on the map, south of Glory Inn, has been destroyed, though some red clay is still seen there.

At Totter Down there are clays.

The Castle on Barbury Hill is Chalk, but on the south-east side there is a small quantity of yellowish brown sandy clay, thickly mixed with angular flints. The top of the ridge running from Hackpen to Barbury Hill is nearly all Chalk, but there a few pot-holes contain a washy sandy clay of a yellowish red or brown colour. Also on the ridge north of Wick Farm there is some drifty looking clay with flints, but the Chalk comes to the surface on the highest points.

A mile to the south-south-east of Barbury Hill, at a plantation by the road side, there are a few pot-holes of yellowish sand and yellowish red clay. In a "chalk well," one side is chalk to the surface, and on the other yellow sands and red clays for more than 12 feet deep.

Near the Barrow, west of Ogbourn St. George, there are yellow clays and sands, much mixed with flints. There are indications here of old pits, as if the clays and sands had been worked.

Besides these clays and sands, nearly the whole surface of the ground is covered by a stratum of angular flints covering alike both Chalk and Tertiary strata, and when genuine Tertiary beds are below the flints are generally mixed with red clay. It is through this angular flint stratum that the farmer sinks pits, or (as they are called in this country) "chalk-wells," from which they extract chalk for the purpose of spreading it over the flinty surface of the ground.

I may remark, in conclusion, that the sites of the Tertiary outliers are well marked, by being either covered with wood, or else by the ground being under cultivation, thus forming a strong contrast to the open downs of the higher Chalk formation.

Druid Stones, Sarsen Stones, or Grey Wethers.—In many places the surface of the Chalk is strewn with blocks of hard siliceous grit, known as Druid stones, Sarsen stones, and Grey Wethers. On Marlborough Downs, and the country to the south near Marlborough and Fyfield, they are especially numerous, and the walls by the turnpike road are built of, and the roads mended with them. Elsewhere on Marlborough Downs they are broken by the hammer into rectangular blocks for paving stones. A few of the places where they are most numerous are marked "large stones" on the Ordnance map, but these yield no idea of their surprising number, or of the extent of ground they cover, no indication being given of their occurrence over many large areas, where they strew the ground so thickly that across miles of country a person might almost leap from stone to stone without touching the ground on which they lie. Many of these flat masses of grey grit are four or five yards across, and they are often about four feet in thickness. Some of them have little basins on their flat surfaces, similar to the hollows made on rocks on sea shores by the gyration of stones set in motion by the waves.

In the present state of our knowledge, their distribution seems somewhat capricious. South of Piggle Dean they thickly strew the west slope of the valley, the east slope being bare. Further up they rise on the east side of the valley on Overton Down, and ascending the slope they gradually get smaller and more sparingly distributed. In the next valley, near Broughton Copse, they lie in great profusion, stretching northwards towards Toller Down, where they are found, but sparingly *upon* the Plastic Clay. On Hackpen they also lie on the surface of the same Tertiary outlier, they occur in quantities on the Upper Chalk of Marlborough Downs in the valleys east of Hackpen, and in the country mapped in the neighbouring Sheet. On the Chalk Downs north of the Vale of Pewsey they strew the surface of many of the valleys in prodigious quantities. On the high Downs of the Upper Chalk east and north-east of Ogbourn St. Andrew's, they are comparatively rare. West of Marlborough Downs there are few or none on the steep flank of Hackpen by the brick kilns, but they occasionally strew the minor valleys that indent the flank of this hill, as, for instance, where a small *stream of stones* lies in the bottom of the valley of Monkton Down. On the broad plain of the Lower Chalk they are scattered on the ground towards Avebury, gradually decreasing in number to the west. The huge masses of the temple of Avebury were probably transported by the Druids from the adjacent Downs on which they were originally deposited as part of the Tertiary strata.

The *Grey Wethers* lying in places on the Plastic Clay, there is reason to believe that they belong to or else are of later date than that formation. In their present disjointed state it is also clear that they are only the fragments of a stratum which had a very wide range, which there is reason to believe, along with other Eocene strata, spread over the Chalk Downs of the west of of England. That the Lower Eocene strata once extended over broad areas of the Chalk, from which it has been stripped by denudation, is evident from the fact, that in many cases outliers of Plastic Clay, and small portions preserved in pot-holes, are scattered over the Chalk, and sometimes occur on the very verge of the Upper Chalk escarpment. It is most improbable, or rather impossible, that under these circumstances the original edge of the Eocene beds ran along the edge of the present escarpment; and the conclusion seems inevitable, that along with the Chalk the Eocene beds have been denuded away from above the Oolitic strata that lie on the north-west. The presence of many large and small masses of the Grey Wethers on the surface of the Oolitic plains near Swindon, and far beyond, would in this manner be easily accounted for, and also the circumstance that below the Chalk escarpment they are often apt to be less angular and more waterworn than the slab-like blocks on the Downs, the reason being that they were probably much more subjected to the influences of marine denudation during oscillations of level, much of the Oolitic plains being below water, when the chalk escarpment formed a late Tertiary line of coast cliff.

The Rev. W. D. Conybeare, in a letter published in the "Gentleman's Magazine" (1833, vol. 103, part ii., p. 452), identifies the large stones of the second and outermost circles of Stonehenge (trilithons) with the Grey Wethers "scattered over the chalky downs of Wiltshire, so that the immediate vicinity may have afforded any quantity and of any size required." This first settled the point as to the derivation of the larger stones used in the construction of Stonehenge and Avebury. The smaller stones in two of the inner circles of Stonehenge he also correctly states are chiefly greenstone, which must have been brought from a distance,—he conjectures from Ireland. They are certainly not drifted boulders, and do not resemble the igneous rocks of Charnwood Forest, and without asserting that they came from Wales or Shropshire, I may state that they are of the same nature as the igneous rocks of part of the Lower Silurian region of North Pembrokeshire, of Caernarvonshire, and of the Llandeilo flag district of Montgomeryshire, &c., west of the Stiper Stones. The so-called altar-stone is a slab of felspathic hornstone, a rock plentiful in the districts above cited.

It has been pointed out by Mr. Prestwich that the evidence respecting the saccharoid rocks, termed Druid sandstones, as it now stands is in favour of these rocks having been derived from the Plastic Clay, or, according to his nomenclature, from the Woolwich and Reading series. He arrived at this conclusion from the circumstance that though "it is very rarely that solidified portions of the strata are found in situ," still "in the western part of the London Tertiary district the middle division of the lower Tertiaries always contains more or less extensive beds of quartzose sand, with patches or layers of pebbles in the lower part, more especially, of the group, while patches of sub-angular flints are also occasionally met with; consequently we have the elements necessary to produce the required results whenever circumstances, as might easily happen, occurred to consolidate the materials." In accordance with this view he finds that wherever the stones are most numerous, there the nearest Tertiary strata, even though unconsolidated, are apt to assume a similar sandy or pebbly character. This helps to account for the patchy distribution of the Grey Wethers around Tertiary areas since where they do not occur we may suppose, that though the Chalk was there also covered by Tertiary strata, yet these strata did not there contain the materials by the consolidation of which Grey Wethers were formed.* It seems probable that the Grey Wethers belong to the more compact siliceous patches of the Lower Sandy Tertiary strata, and possibly they further hardened on exposure to external influences when the softer Tertiary material with which they were originally surrounded was denuded away.

Newer Pliocene Drift.—Under this head may be classed two very distinct deposits, the older belonging to the period of the Northern Drift, the more recent having been formed

* Prestwich, Journal of the Geological Society, vol. x., p. 123, 1853.

when the surface of the country was submerged to a depth of 500 feet, and when the sea surrounded the more elevated portions of the Cotteswold Hills, and spread over the lower grounds of the Oxford Clay, Kimmeridge Clay, and Gault, which occupy the district between the Great Oolite and the Chalk escarpment.

The Northern Drift is represented by erratic pebbles of quartz, grit, and hornstone, which are freely scattered over the district included between a line drawn from Cirencester to Castle Combe on the one side, and the upper escarpment of the Chalk on the other. The course of these pebbles may be traced to the Valley of Moreton, and there connected with the sands and gravels of the Glacial or Northern Drift period. Northward of the line here indicated erratic pebbles do not extend; and as a rule, the Cotteswold promontory, and the high westerly margin of the range, are exempt from their presence.

Flint Gravel.—There is another class of high level gravel, which we find capping the upper gravel on the Oxford clay, composed almost exclusively of chalk flints, and which, having spread and been derived from the waste of the Chalk, have travelled in a direction opposite to that of the quartz pebbles. Nevertheless it is highly probable they are contemporaneous, as in the neighbourhood of Oxford, flint and quartzose gravel are intimately associated; and we can well understand a shingle beach of flints extending from the old chalk cliffs towards the south becoming mixed with pebbles transported by tides or currents from the north.

The flint gravel may be seen at Flintham Hill near Oaksey; by the turnpike road at Flisterage, near Minety; on the hill tops of the Oxford clay around Malmesbury at Rodborne, and Buscot Park near Farringdon. These localities are all about 600 feet above the sea level.

Estuarine Gravel.—The gravel of this period may readily be distinguished from that just described, in being composed for the most part of Oolitic detritus, and from the fact of its occupying lower levels. This gravels is generally formed of small and well rounded pebbles; and from the general resemblance it bears to that in Stroud Valley, both as to position and character, it may be considered as belonging to the same period. This gravel may be viewed at Broughton Poggs, Lechlade, and along the turnpike road between that town and Fairford; at Horcott Hill, Maisey Hampton, where it reaches an unusually high elevation; at Amney Park, South Cerney, east of Chelworth, and near Eastcourt, near Crudwell, and in fragments in the lower grounds around Malmesbury.

UNIV.
GEOLOGIE
GENT

LONDON:
Printed by GEORGE E. EYRE and WILLIAM SPOTTISWOODE,
Printers to the Queen's most Excellent Majesty.
For Her Majesty's Stationery Office.

www.ingramcontent.com/pod-product-compliance
Lightning Source LLC
LaVergne TN
LVHW012010160826
845678LV00002B/755